Thankfulness: A Gratitude Attitude!

by Liz George

Content Consultant

Samantha Gambino, Psy.D.
Licensed Psychologist, New York, New York

Reading Consultant

Jeanne M. Clidas, Ph.D.
Reading Specialist

Children's Press®
An Imprint of Scholastic Inc.

Library of Congress Cataloging-in-Publication Data
George, Liz, author.
  Thankfulness : a gratitude attitude / by Liz George.
    pages cm. -- (Rookie talk about it)
  Summary: "Teaches the reader about thankfulness."-- Provided by publisher.
  ISBN 978-0-531-21514-2 (library binding) -- ISBN 978-0-531-21382-7 (pbk.)
  1. Gratitude--Juvenile literature. 2. Conduct of life--Juvenile literature. I. Title.

BJ1533.G8G46 2016
179.9--dc23   2015018084

Produced by Spooky Cheetah Press
Design by Keith Plechaty

Printed in China 62

SCHOLASTIC, CHILDREN'S PRESS, ROOKIE TALK ABOUT IT™, and associated logos
are trademarks and/or registered trademarks of Scholastic Inc.

1 2 3 4 5 6 7 8 9 10 R 25 24 23 22 21 20 19 18 17 16

Photographs ©: cover: Jenna Adesso; 3 top: sevenke/Shutterstock, Inc.; 3 bottom:
Anson0618/Shutterstock, Inc.; 4: Fabio Cardoso/Masterfile/Corbis Images; 7:
holbox/Shutterstock, Inc.; 8: Christopher Robbins/Getty Images; 11: Monkey Business
Images/Shutterstock, Inc.; 12: Fuse/Thinkstock; 15: Media Bakery; 16: Monkey Business
Images/Shutterstock, Inc.; 19: Andresr/Shutterstock, Inc.; 20: Fuse/Thinkstock; 23:
ParkerDeen/iStockphoto; 24: Steve Debenport/iStockphoto; 27: BFA/SIPA/Newscom;
28: JR Carvey/Streetfly Studio/Media Bakery; 29: Sonya Farrell/Media Bakery; 30:
Huntstock/Thinkstock; 31 top: Media Bakery; 31 center top: Masterfile; 31 center
bottom: Steve Debenport/iStockphoto; 31 bottom: sevenke/Shutterstock, Inc.

Table of Contents

What Is Thankfulness?

Imagine you are having trouble with your homework. Your big sister offers to help. You feel really good inside. That great feeling is thankfulness.

You feel thankfulness when you think about the things in your life that make you happy. Those might be small things, like a sunny day. Or they can be big things, like the people or pets you love. Thankfulness is also called **gratitude**.

Try it!

Make a list of all the things you are thankful for. Keep it someplace where you will be sure to see it every day.

A Gratitude Attitude

Gratitude is an attitude that feels good. Thankfulness helps you **appreciate** what you have.

It is hard to be thankful all the time—like when you had a really bad day. But remembering to be thankful can even make a bad day feel better!

To practice a gratitude attitude,
you can:

- Turn **disappointment** around.
  When things are not going well, find
  something to look forward to.

- Be mindful. Notice all the little things
  you have to be grateful for.

- Remember to show your gratitude!
  That makes others feel good, too.

On the next few pages, you can read about some kids who try to have a gratitude attitude. You have probably been in the same situations they have. When you read their stories, ask yourself, "How would I feel?"

Liam is disappointed because his friend cannot come over to play. Then he remembers that his grandfather is coming to visit this weekend. He imagines the fun he will have then. He starts to feel better.

Try it! What does Liam do to feel thankful?

Try it!

What does Emily's family teach Mason about thankfulness?

Mason is having dinner at his friend Emily's house. Everyone in Emily's family shares something they are thankful for that day.

Her mom says she is thankful for the food they have to eat. Emily was happy to see a butterfly at recess. Mason is thankful for having such a good friend.

Amelia wants to play with her friends. But first she has to finish her chores. Amelia's brother Wyatt offers to help. They get the work done fast.

Amelia draws a picture of Wyatt and writes: "Thanks to the best brother ever." She has made Wyatt feel really good!

Try it! How does Amelia show her thankfulness?

Passing It On

Thankfulness works two ways. It is good to say "thank you." It is also nice to be thanked by others. Be thankful for all you have. Then look for ways to help others.

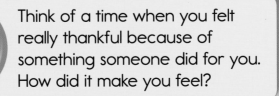

Try it! Think of a time when you felt really thankful because of something someone did for you. How did it make you feel?

Passing it on can be as simple as helping people you know. Pick a job that is just right for you. You might help your neighbor carry her groceries. Or you could shovel the walk for her after it snows. You will find that helping others makes you feel good, too!

You can also pass it on to people you do not even know. Think about all you have to be thankful for. There are others who might not have as much.

Ask an adult to help you give clothes you have outgrown to a local shelter. Or you can **donate** food to a food bank.

Having a gratitude attitude makes everyone feel good!

Neha Gupta

Neha Gupta is thankful for everything that she has. She showed her gratitude by giving to others who have less.

Neha grew up in Pennsylvania. Her parents are from India. Every year, they visited India. They brought gifts to children in a local orphanage. One visit, when Neha was nine years old, changed her life.

Neha saw little girls sleeping on dirt floors. It struck her how much she had and how little they had.

When she returned home, Neha organized a neighborhood tag sale. She raised $700 for the children in the orphanage. The money was used for a library, food, clothes, and blankets.

A few years later, with her parents' help, Neha started Empower Orphans. The organization has raised more than $1.3 million for education, computer labs, clean water, and much more. Being thankful helped Neha become a 2014 International Children's Peace Prize Winner.

You can bring more thankfulness into your life by making a Gratitude Jar:

You will need: a label; colored markers; a clean, empty jar; construction paper; and scissors.

1. Write "Gratitude Jar" on the label. Attach it to the front of the jar.

2. Cut out squares of paper. Write down things you are thankful for on each. Place the notes in the jar. Ask family members to add their notes, too.

3. Read the notes often and continue to add more. This will help remind you to be thankful for all that you have.

What Would You Do?

Read the story below and imagine what you might do in this situation.

It is your day to share in class. You talk about the awesome fair your parents took you to. Your teacher points out how nice it was of your parents to plan such a special day. You realize you never actually thanked them.

Need help getting started?

- How might you show your thankfulness to your parents? Can you write them a note or draw a picture for them?

- Is there something else you can do for your parents to show them your appreciation?

29

How Thankful Are You?

1. During the day, you say "thank you":

    a. not at all.

    b. one or two times.

    c. every time someone gives you something or helps you.

2. When you think about it, you are thankful for:

    a. not much.

    b. your favorite toys.

    c. so many things—including the people you love.

3. Your aunt buys you a great birthday gift. You:

    a. say a quick "thanks" as you open it and then set it aside. There are more gifts to open!

    b. stop to give her a thank-you hug.

    c. send her a thank-you note telling her how much fun you had when you played with the toy.

Answer key: A: 1 point, B: 2 points, C: 3 points

If you scored 9 points, you have a real gratitude attitude! If you scored 3-8 points, try to start noticing moments when you can feel thankful and express it, too.

Glossary

appreciate (ah-PREE-shee-ayt): understand how important something or someone is

disappointment (diss-uh-POINT-ment): feeling of being let down

donate (DOH-nayt): give something to someone who needs it

gratitude (GRAT-uh-tood): feeling of being thankful and grateful for things

Index

Facts for Now

Visit this Scholastic Web site for more information on thankfulness:
www.factsfornow.scholastic.com
Enter the keyword **Thankfulness**

About the Author

Liz George is a writer and a licensed psychotherapist. She lives in Montclair, New Jersey, with her husband, Rob, her son, Zack, and her daughter, Ava. Liz enjoys helping teenagers get in touch with their feelings.